DIY FOR BOYS

THE SUPERSPY HANDBOOK

Secret-compartment book

Fingerprint powder

Top Secret Message

by Ruth Owen

Invisible ink

PowerKiDS press.

New York

Published in 2014 by The Rosen Publishing Group, Inc.
29 East 21st Street, New York, NY 10010

Produced for Rosen by Ruby Tuesday Books Ltd
Editor for Ruby Tuesday Books Ltd: Mark J. Sachner
US Editor: Joshua Shadowens
Designers: Tammy West and Emma Randall

With special thanks to Steve Owen for his help in developing and making
the projects in this book.

Photo Credits:
Cover, 1, 6—7, 8—9, 10—11, 16—17, 18—19, 20—21, 22—23, 24—25, 28—29
© Ruby Tuesday Books and John Such; cover, 1, 3, 4—5, 6—7, 12—13, 14—15,
19, 20—21, 22—23, 24—25, 26—27, 28—29 © Shutterstock.

Library of Congress Cataloging-in-Publication Data

Owen, Ruth, 1967—
 The superspy handbook / Ruth Owen.
     pages cm — (DIY for boys)
 Includes index.
 ISBN 978-1-4777-6282-0 (library binding) — ISBN 978-1-4777-6283-7 (pbk.) —
 ISBN 978-1-4777-6284-4 (6-pack)
 1. Espionage—Equipment and supplies—Juvenile literature. I. Title. II. Title: Super
spy handbook.
 UB270.5.O943 2014
 327.120028'4—dc23
                              2013035228

Manufactured in the United States of America

CPSIA Compliance Information: Batch #W14PK8 For Further Information contact: Rosen Publishing, New York, New York at 1-800-237-9932

CONTENTS

WARNING!

Neither the author nor the publisher shall be liable for any bodily harm or damage to property that may happen as a result of carrying out the activities in this book.

WHAT IS A SPY?

A spy is a person whose job it is to find out secret information. A spy must do this without the person or organization that holds that information ever finding out.

To be a good spy, you must be intelligent, sneaky, and **stealthy**. If your target discovers you are spying on him or her, you will have failed your **mission**.

A spy must be able to plan ahead. If a mission goes wrong, however, you must be able to think fast to get yourself out of trouble.

Sometimes a spy works with a partner or team of other spies. To communicate with your fellow spies, you will have to send secret messages and use **codes**. You will also need some top spy **gadgets** to help you on your missions.

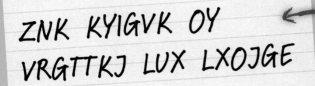

ZNK KYIGVK OY
VRGTTKJ LUX LXOJGE

A spy must be able to write secret messages.

Following a suspect while staying out of sight is an essential spy skill.

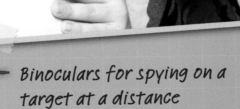

Binoculars for spying on a target at a distance

Always carry a notebook and pen to record everything you find out.

When on a mission, you may have to spend time spying on a particular suspect.

This could involve shadowing that person, which means following him or her, without your target realizing you are there.

Binoculars are the right tool for distance spying.

You might also be on **surveillance**. This could mean watching a suspect from a distance using binoculars, or needing to see over walls, around buildings, or into a window while staying out of view. To see into a place while staying hidden, you need to use a gadget called a periscope.

For looking over walls while staying out of view, you need a periscope.

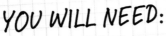

YOU WILL NEED:

- 2 small make-up mirrors
- A large piece of cardboard
- A pencil and ruler
- A craft knife
- A hot glue gun
- Twigs and leaves for camouflage as required

Make-up mirror

STEP 1:

Measure the two make-up mirrors. You will make your periscope to fit the size of the mirrors. For example, the instructions below allow for each mirror measuring 2 inches (5 cm) by 1 inch (2.5 cm). If your mirrors are bigger or smaller, adjust the dimensions of the periscope plan to fit.

STEP 2:

Draw the plan below onto a large piece of cardboard.

Cardboard that's about the thickness of a cereal box is the easiest to work with.

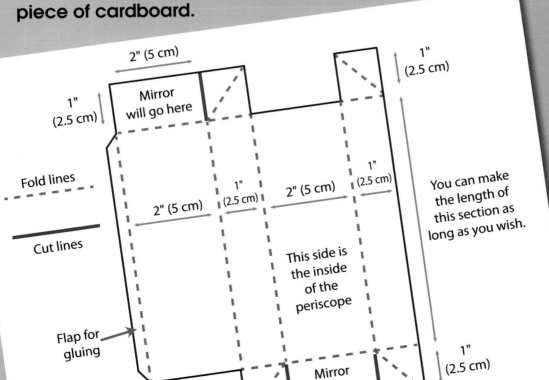

2" (5 cm)

1" (2.5 cm)

1" (2.5 cm)

Mirror will go here

Fold lines

- - - - -

Cut lines

1" (2.5 cm)

2" (5 cm)

2" (5 cm)

1" (2.5 cm)

2" (5 cm)

1" (2.5 cm)

You can make the length of this section as long as you wish.

This side is the inside of the periscope

Flap for gluing

Mirror will go here

1" (2.5 cm)

STEP 3:
Cut along the three cut lines as marked.

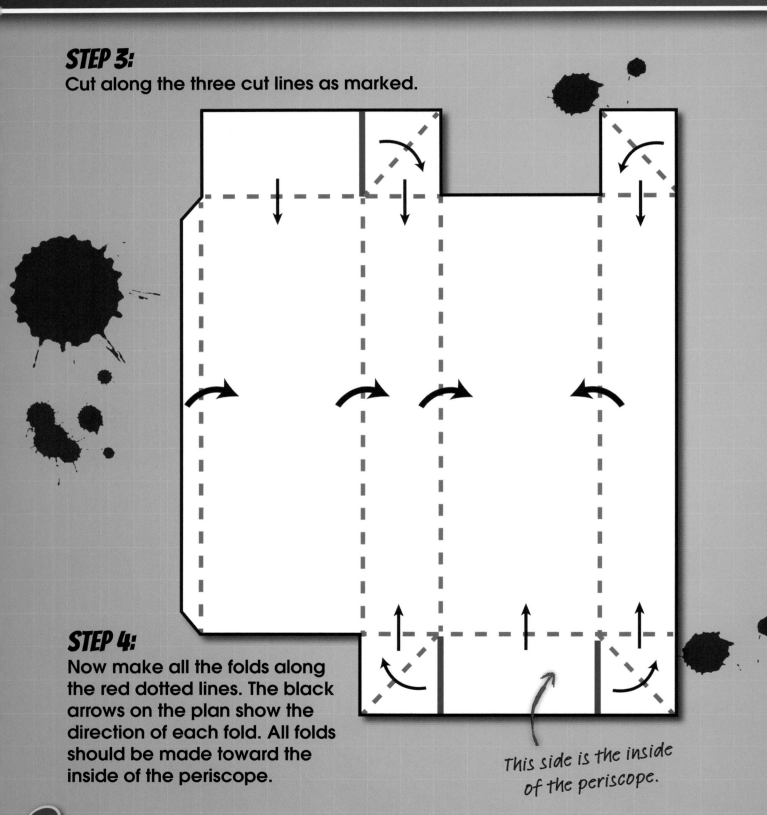

STEP 4:
Now make all the folds along the red dotted lines. The black arrows on the plan show the direction of each fold. All folds should be made toward the inside of the periscope.

This side is the inside of the periscope.

STEP 5:

Once all your folds and cuts are ready, glue the mirrors in place using a hot glue gun.

Mirror

Mirror

STEP 6:

Now squeeze glue onto the inside of the gluing flap, fold the body of the periscope into a rectangular tube, and press down on the flap so it sticks the tube together.

The ends of the tube will look like this.

STEP 7:

Now, position one of the mirrors so it is roughly at a 45 degree angle and tuck one side edge of the mirror into the fold of one of the square flaps of cardboard. Glue or tape the square cardboard flap to the back of the mirror.

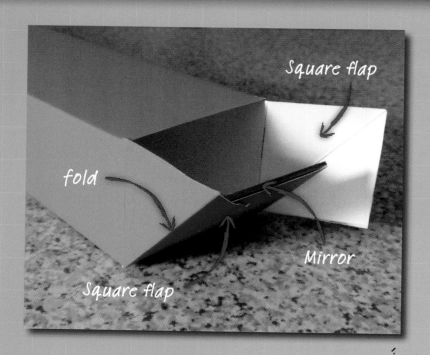

Square flap

fold

Mirror

Square flap

STEP 8:

Repeat with the second square flap of cardboard. The end of the periscope should now look like this, with the mirror firmly held at a 45 degree angle.

STEP 9:

Repeat steps 7 and 8 at the other end of the periscope. The finished periscope should now look like this.

And if you turn it over, like this.

STEP 10:

When using the periscope, hold it upright so that you can look into a mirror at the bottom, while the top mirror is directed at your target.

STEP 11:

If you will be using your periscope outdoors where there are plants, you can add camouflage. Paint your periscope green, or use green cardboard. Glue leaves and twigs onto the periscope to help it blend in with a natural environment.

You are hiding down here

If you hide among shrubs and other plants, your camouflaged periscope will be almost invisible.

Periscope

INVISIBLE INK MESSAGES

Spies must communicate with fellow spies and the organization they are working for.

To pass messages to each other, spies often use pre-arranged places called "dead drops." One spy leaves a message in a dead drop, such as a tree hole. Then a second spy picks it up.

If your message should accidentally fall into enemy hands, though, it must be impossible to read. If you write the message in invisible ink, it will look just like a piece of blank paper. Your spying partner will know how to reveal the secret information it contains, though. Learn how to make an invisible ink message by following these instructions.

YOU WILL NEED:
- A lemon
- A knife
- A cutting board
- A small bowl
- Paper
- Cotton swabs
- An iron and ironing board

Dead drop

STEP 1:

Cut a lemon in half, and then squeeze all the juice from both halves into the bowl.

WARNING:

Only use a knife if an adult is there to help you.

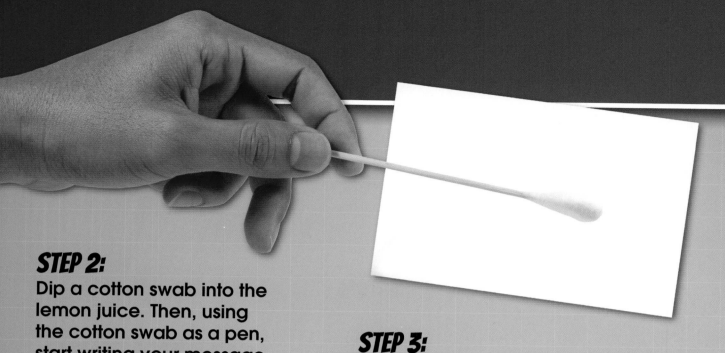

STEP 2:

Dip a cotton swab into the lemon juice. Then, using the cotton swab as a pen, start writing your message in lemon juice.

STEP 3:

When you've finished writing your message, allow the lemon juice to dry. The message will be invisible on the paper.

STEP 4:

Now pass the message to a fellow spy. You can use a dead drop for added security.

No one can tell there's a secret message hidden between these two books!

STEP 5:

To reveal a message made in lemon juice invisible ink, you need an iron. Turn the iron on to a medium heat.

STEP 6:

When the iron is heated, place the paper onto a heat-resistant surface such as an ironing board.

WARNING:

Only use an iron if an adult is there to help you.

Secret message before ironing

Code = 2535

Secret message after ironing

STEP 7:

Hold the hot iron onto the paper for about 5 seconds, then lift the iron off. Keep ironing the paper in 5-second bursts. The lemon juice message will gradually appear.

By ironing the paper in 5-second bursts, you will be applying enough heat to the lemon juice to reveal the message, but the paper will not burn.

SECRET SPY CODES

One of the safest ways to pass the secrets you've discovered to a fellow spy, or to your spy agency, is to use a code.

First, you must decide on a message. Then, using your code, you will **encrypt** your message. Your spying partner will share the same code as you and will therefore be able to decode your message when he or she receives it. If an enemy **intercepts** your message, however, all that person will see is mixed-up letters, numbers, or symbols that will be meaningless to them.

In order to send messages using a code, you and your spying partner must each make a gadget called a cipher wheel.

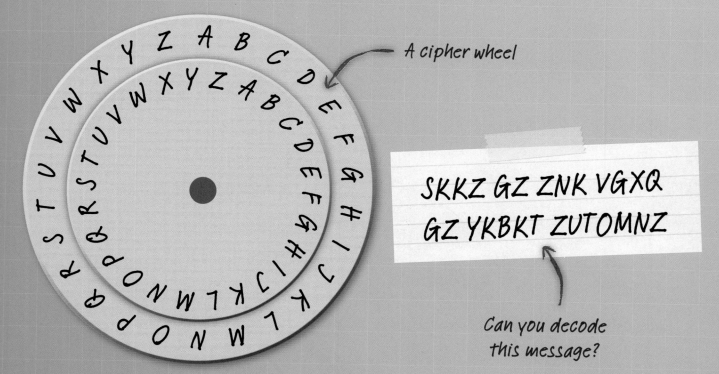

A cipher wheel

SKKZ GZ ZNK VGXQ
GZ YKBKT ZUTOMNZ

Can you decode
this message?

STEP 1:
Cut two circles from the cardboard. One circle should be smaller and fit inside the larger one.

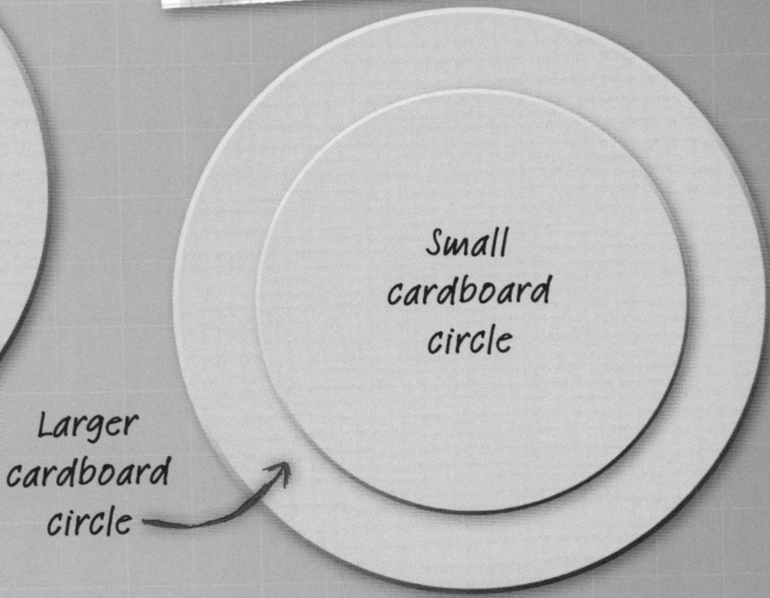

YOU WILL NEED:
- Cardboard
- Scissors
- A marker
- A paper fastener

Small cardboard circle

Larger cardboard circle

STEP 2:
Write the letters of the alphabet around the outside of the larger circle.

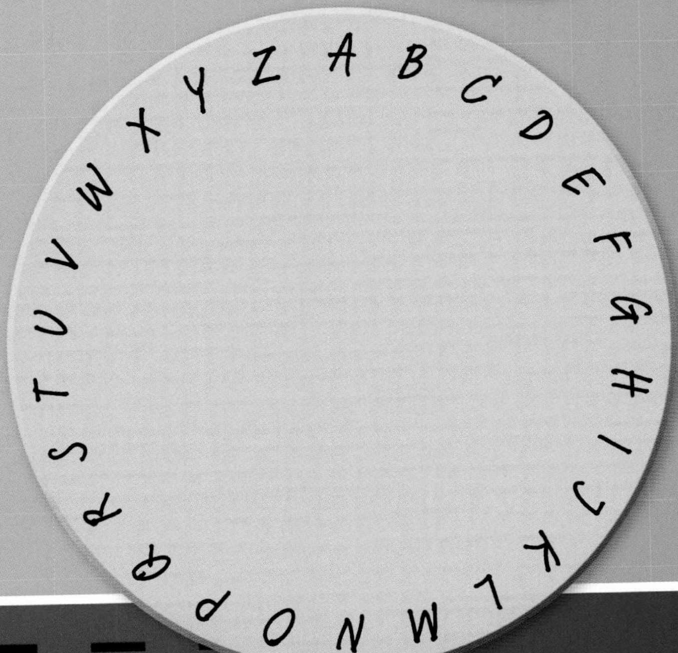

A B C D E F G H I J K L M N O P Q R S T U V W X Y Z

STEP 3:
Using a paper fastener, pin the small circle inside the large circle.

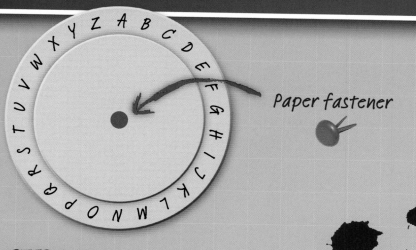

Paper fastener

STEP 4:
Now write the letters of the alphabet around the outside of the small circle. Make sure they neatly line up with the outer circle of letters.

The cipher wheel is now ready to use.

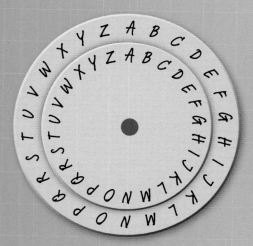

G is the key letter

STEP 5:
To use the wheel to encrypt and decode messages, you must first choose one letter from the inner circle to be the key letter. For example, if the letter G is the key letter, you turn the inner wheel so that G is below A.

STEP 6:
Both you and your spying partner must know what the key letter is. Tell no one!

STEP 7:

Now, when writing a message, the letter A becomes G. The letter P becomes V and so on. So the word APPLE would look like this written in your code:

APPLE

GVVRK

STEP 8:

Using the cipher wheel, the message on page 16 is decoded as follows:

SKKZ GZ ZNK VGXQ

MEET AT THE PARK

GZ YKBKT ZUTOMNZ

AT SEVEN TONIGHT

STEP 9:

To make your coded messages look even more complicated, you can add numbers or even symbols to the inner ring.

STEP 10:

You can even make a tiny, pocket-sized cipher wheel to carry with you on missions!

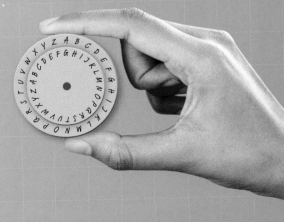

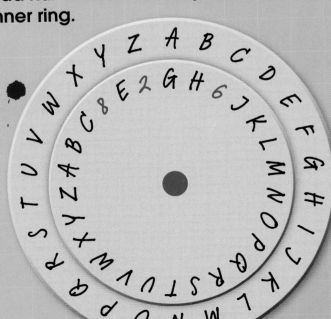

CONFIDENTIAL COOKIES

As a spy, you never know what you will be required to do next. Wear a disguise, shadow a suspect, and even bake!

Yes, you read that right. One of the best ways to pass information to fellow spies in a crowded room, right under the noses of the enemy, is in their food. If your spying partners are being held prisoner (or have been grounded), you might also be allowed to take them some food. Your enemies won't suspect that the delicious cookies you offer to your spying partners contain **confidential** messages!

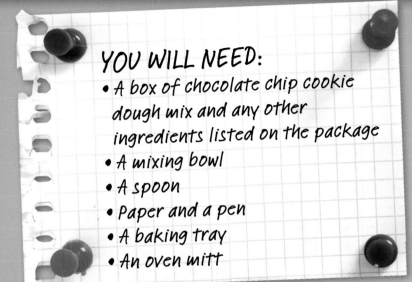

YOU WILL NEED:
- A box of chocolate chip cookie dough mix and any other ingredients listed on the package
- A mixing bowl
- A spoon
- Paper and a pen
- A baking tray
- An oven mitt

STEP 1:
Prepare the cookie dough following the instructions on the packet. Take large spoonfuls of the dough and mold them into balls with your hands.

STEP 2:

Write your secret message on a tiny piece of paper. Then fold up the message and push it deep into the center of a ball of cookie dough.

ZNK KYIGVK OY VRGTTKJ LUX LXOJGE

Cookie containing message

STEP 3:

Place the cookies on a baking tray and bake according to the instructions on the package. Put your confidential cookie in one corner of the tray so you remember which one it is.

STEP 4:

When the cookies are baked, remove the baking tray from the oven using the oven mitt. Allow the cookies to cool.

STEP 5:

It will be impossible for anyone to tell there is a note inside the cookie. When a spying partner breaks open the cookie or bites into it, however, he or she will find the message.

SECRET-COMPARTMENT BOOK

When you're on a mission, it's important that you remain **undercover** and that any information you discover does not fall into enemy hands.

If enemy spies search your hideout (or bedroom), they must not find any gadgets, messages from fellow spies, or any clues as to what you are doing. Therefore, it's essential that you have a secure hiding place for all your most important spy equipment.

Follow these instructions to make a book with a secret compartment. When it is placed on a bookshelf with other books, no one will suspect what's really between the book's covers.

Who would guess this book contains top-secret information!

STEP 1:

Open up the book a few pages in. On the right-hand page draw a rectangle the size you want your secret compartment to be.

Make sure you leave at least a 1-inch (2.5-cm) border around the secret compartment. This will ensure that the book stays rigid.

A book with a hard cover

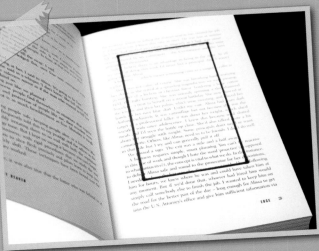

Keep the cover and left-hand pages clean of glue by covering them with plastic wrap.

STEP 2:

Now take the book's back cover, front cover, and the pages on the left-hand side and cover them with plastic wrap to keep them clean.

STEP 3:

Carefully brush the glue and water mix around the edges of all the right-hand pages. This will glue the pages together and help keep the book rigid.

Brush glue on the ends of the pages at the top, bottom, and right-hand side of the book.

STEP 4:

Allow the glue to dry. When the glue dries, it will be completely see-through, and the ends of the pages will look like a normal book.

STEP 5:

Using a craft knife, carefully cut along the marked edge of the secret compartment. Don't try to cut all the way through the book at once. Cut just a few pages at a time, and gradually cut deeper into the book.

STEP 6:

Don't cut all the way through to the back cover, but leave some complete pages behind the secret compartment, again to help keep the book rigid.

STEP 7:

Your secret-compartment book can now be used for storing money, keys, a cell phone, gadgets, coded messages, or anything you don't want to fall into enemy hands!

STEP 8:

If you need a secret hiding place for small pieces of equipment, you can cut a secret compartment into a deck of playing cards. Leave just a few cards uncut to place on the top and bottom of the pack.

The loose cards can be held in place with rubber bands.

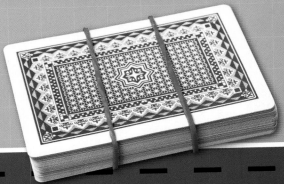

A deck of cards with a secret compartment is the perfect way to keep small items hidden when traveling.

FINGERPRINT POWDER

Once you have followed a suspect to a location, you might want to collect proof that he or she was at that place. Alternatively, if you believe enemy spies have found your hide-out, you will want to look for **evidence** that they were there.

One way to prove a suspect was at a specific location is to find that person's fingerprints. If someone's fingers or thumbs touch an object or surface, fingerprints made of sweat and oil are left behind. Everyone's fingerprints are **unique**, so they prove that a person was in a particular place.

It's possible to collect a fingerprint using fingerprint powder. Here's how to make your own powder by mixing soot and corn starch.

STEP 1:

To make some soot, place a candle firmly into a candleholder. Light the candle.

YOU WILL NEED:

- A candle and candleholder
- Matches
- A ceramic cup
- A teaspoon
- A small bowl
- Corn starch
- A small jar with a lid
- A magnifying glass
- Clear sticky tape
- White cardboard

STEP 2:

Hold the ceramic cup over the candle so the flame is touching the inside bottom of the cup. Soot will start to form inside the cup.

WARNING!
Only light a candle and make soot if an adult is there to help you.

STEP 3:

As soot forms, use a teaspoon to scrape it from the cup into a small bowl. Try to collect about a teaspoon of soot. Be patient, because this will take some time.

STEP 4:

Once you've collected some soot, stir a tiny amount of corn starch into the soot. Keep adding small amounts of corn starch until the mixture becomes a dark gray color.

Remember: You can add more corn starch, but you can't take it back out if you put in too much at the start.

Corn starch

Soot mixed with corn starch

STEP 5:

Once your fingerprint powder is dark gray, it is ready. Store the powder in a small jar with a lid.

STEP 6:

When you find an item that you suspect an enemy has touched, such as a glass or shiny table top, look carefully for fingerprints with a magnifying glass.

STEP 7:

If you spot a print, sprinkle fingerprint powder over the print. The powder will stick to the print. Gently blow away any excess powder.

Fingerprint powder

Fingerprint

Excess powder

STEP 8:

To save the fingerprint, cover it with sticky tape, then lift up the print and stick the tape to a piece of white cardboard. Hide the fingerprint in a safe place. It could be useful evidence for the future!

codes (KOHDZ)
Words, letters, numbers, or symbols that are used to represent others in order to create a secret message or some other kind of secret text.

confidential (KON-fih-dent-shul)
Kept secret.

encrypt (in-KRIPT)
To convert into a code.

evidence (EH-vuh-dunts)
Proof or disproof, such as a fingerprint that proves a person touched a particular object and was therefore in a particular place.

gadgets (GA-juts)
Mechanical or electronic devices that do a specific job. Often a gadget is very small.

intercepts (in-ter-SEPTS)
Stops the movement of something or somebody from one place to another.

mission (MIH-shun)
An important assignment or task.

stealthy (STEL-thee)
Careful and secretive, so as to avoid detection.

surveillance (sur-VAY-lunts)
Keeping watch over someone or something.

undercover (un-dur-KUH-vur)
In disguise or doing something secretly.

unique (yoo-NEEK)
One of a kind.

WEBSITES

Due to the changing nature of Internet links, Powerkids Press has developed an online list of websites related to the subject of this book. This site is updated regularly. Please use this link to access the list:
www.powerkidslinks.com/dfb/spy/

READ MORE

Martin, Michael. *Spy Gear*. Spies. Mankato, MN: Capstone Press, 2008.

McFadzean, Lesley. *Creating and Cracking Codes*. Discovery Education: Discoveries and Inventions. New York: PowerKids Press, 2013.

Shea, Therese. *Spy Planes*. Military Machines. New York: Gareth Stevens Learning Library, 2013.

INDEX